Say, "Yes!"

Say, "Yes!"

Sandra Williamson

Text copyright © 2014—Sandra Williamson
Illustrations copyright "Warrior Bride" © 2014—Constance Woods
All other illustrations copyright © 2014—Julie A. Johnston

Say, "Yes!": Are you Ready for the Bridegroom's Soon Return?
ISBN 978-0-9911578-0-8
Published by
PALADIN PUBLISHING
P.O. Box 700515
Tulsa, OK 74170

Text Design and Layout: Lisa Simpson

Printed in the United States of America.

Acknowledgement

A special acknowledgement must be made for Julie A. Johnston for her artistic rendition of The Bride. I must express my appreciation for the multiplied hours she spent listening to me recite minute details of the vision in order to formulate a precise mental image, and then meticulously transfer that image onto canvas. When you look at the intricate details of the artwork and place yourself in the vision as His Bride, you will realize, *you* are valuable, His Beloved! Copies of the artwork may be purchased online at: www.GodsER.us.

Also, a special thank you and much appreciation to Constance Woods and Wings of Mercy Art for the use of Warrior Bride, a prophetic rendition of the Bride of Christ used in Chapter 8.

Introduction

A Note to the Male Reader

At first glance, this book seems targeted to a female audience, yet it contains spiritual treasure for all readers. I ask you to forget male/female roles and look at the purpose of the Call of the Lord on your life. This book has nothing to do with sexuality, although it is filled with passion. It has nothing to do with being male, or being female, in the anatomical sense. It has everything to do with authority, purpose, posture, and response. From God's perspective, it encompasses every phase of the life and development of His people.

If you are so masculine that you cannot imagine being called part of the Bride of Christ, imagine yourself in "His Army". For you, let's call it a book about "His Called", in the Army of God.

It is my belief that if the Lord had given this vision to a male, then it would be a story of a private being drafted into His Service. Even as a man's man is attracted to "sign on" with the armed forces, he begins his role as a private, airman, or otherwise. So you will see that the assignment as the Bride is not much different. The inductee must remove his civilian clothes, don his uniform, take up his weapons, and become transformed into a new identity before he is positioned and ranked. From there, new rank is attained by each "Yes sir!" that is carried out. As the finale, you are allowed to enter the battle of your dreams!

In that instance, there would be instruction to the female that what she was about to read applied to her as well. Because in His service, there is no male or female, no marriage or giving in marriage. In His sight, we are all "the Called".

His Service is about entering into a life of Authority, Protection, Serving, and always, Triumph.

If you will allow yourself to hear His commands throughout this book, the commands to His Army, you will come away with what He desires you to have. Quite possibly, you will come away with a fuller measure and with greater understanding than your female counterpart.

Give this your "Atten*tion*!!" and you will have the advantage!

If you do, I assure you, you will not be wasting your time reading this book!

To All Readers

As the Lord unveiled this vision to me, I knew that He was talking to His Bride—those of us who are alive and remain true to Him until the day of His coming. His heart of passion and desire for His people was revealed so strongly to me that I immediately recognized His purpose: *Tell My Beloved I am coming for Her.* Receiving this vision kindled an urgency in me to write, prepare, and present this picture of His all-consuming love that He is ready to consummate now, at the end of the Age. The declaration that keeps resounding in my heart is this: *Hurry! There's not much time!*

As you read, please be sure to also read the Scripture passages that are signified as endnotes. The entire vision and the following detailed account have all previously been set forth in Scripture. When we accept these scriptures as His Truth—one by one and moment by moment—our lives will be transformed. And this is just the beginning of the journey!

Will you join me in hearing the Bridegroom's call, in pondering the thoughts of the Bride as she learns to focus solely on her Beloved, and in considering some additional thoughts posed by this author? These three unique perspectives join to create a glorious picture! As this picture unfolds, you will see His ardent desire is that you willingly respond to His invitation and simply *Say, "Yes!"*

Contents

The following
is a Prophetic Vision given by the Lord
for His People on August 4, 2011,
to Sandra Williamson.

Part 1

I

The Bridegroom Beckons

His eyes blazed with passion causing her heart to beat wildly with anticipation and wonder. Could He really be looking at her this way? Could He really just decree that she was His? And she would be His? Really His? Those eyes were truly fixed only on her. Of that, there was no doubt! His piercing gaze bore through her — to the deepest level of her soul. He saw all, and every part of her melted under His penetrating gaze. Truly, truly His desire was for her alone! Even as she became weak and faint in His presence, His demand upon her kept her as she heard Him declare, "You are Mine!!!" and it pierced her to the very marrow of her bones. She could look nowhere else. Her eyes would not wander. Eye to eye, she stayed fixed on Him. Every breath she took was filled with Him, His scent, His sweetness, His love for her…

"Stay with Me!" His eyes cried. "Look at Me!" He demanded with His stare. "Insecurity is unbecoming on My Bride," He gently chastised.

If she looked away, she would lose Him; her greatest prize, the One her soul loved!

She drew a deep breath, and with total resolve, yielded to His possessive stare.

Her fortitude changed. She held her head upright, her eyes reflecting the adoration of her Beloved. Strength and dignity flooded her being and drenched her in the very essence of His likeness. Her lungs filled with

His sweetness and her resolve became sure as her breath drew Him in and she whispered, "I AM HIS! MY BELOVED!"

And she stepped forward …

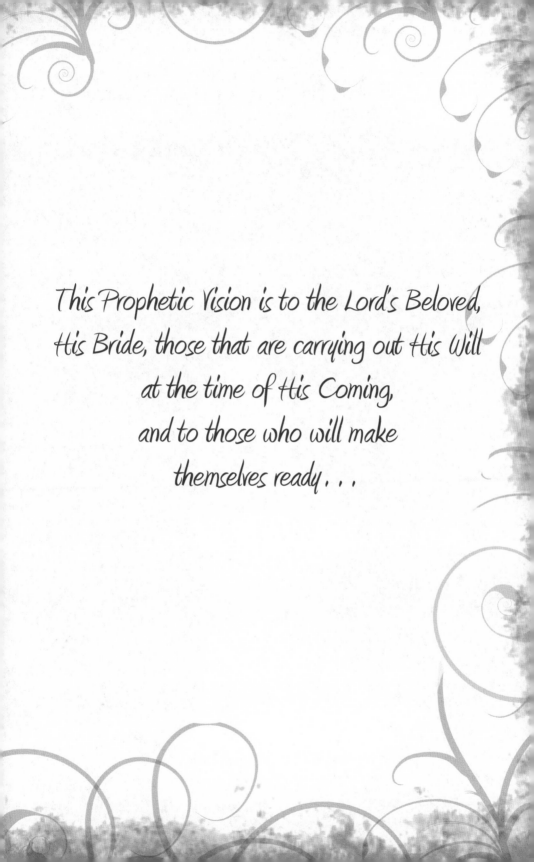

This Prophetic Vision is to the Lord's Beloved,
His Bride, those that are carrying out His Will
at the time of His Coming,
and to those who will make
themselves ready . . .

II

The Vision

He beckoned me to enter through the heavenly veil.[1] The Lord was standing within a four-cornered pavilion[2], like the structures that are situated on the beach at the edge of the sea. The roof and walls, made of a white, chiffon fabric, billowed gently in the breeze. Jesus held open the side of the veil closest to me and invited[3] me in.

I looked around in awe and, although His words were not audible, His thoughts and intentions were as if spoken. He spoke His Peace, He spoke His Love, and He was amused with me. I was looking around, thoroughly enjoying the environment and all the love and peace He was showering upon me. He kept drawing me toward Him. I so enjoyed this intimacy! But only for a moment. Then I looked around and thought, *shouldn't I be doing something?* I knew there was so much work to be done, people to minister to, *shouldn't I be doing something?* The Lord laughed and chuckled. He drew me to Him and communicated to me that I should just rest.[4] But, but…. Just rest? He smiled. Then He beckoned me to rest with Him on a chaise lounge. I realize He really means that I should rest, with Him, right next to Him, peacefully immersed in His presence.[5]

We lay next to each other, He directly behind me, holding me as one holds a child, close and comforting, yet His love was intimate to the heart. I relaxed and enjoyed His presence, and then, again, I thought, *I should be doing something.* He conveyed through His amusement, that I should enjoy this time and rest. I tried to rest, but I was flighty of thought and fidgety. Gently but firmly, the Lord put His arm around me and placed His hand directly through my chest and upon my heart. He began to massage my heart to beat in rhythm with His. Our hearts beat as one! This was amazing! I instantly entered into His rest.[6]

From beyond the veil at the opposite end of the pavilion, I heard a voice say, "The rain[7] of God is coming down! Blood and water!"[8] Jesus stood and took me by the hand. He led me through the pavilion and as we reached the opposite side, He removed the veil. What I saw fascinated me — there was wave upon wave of golden mist, floating down from the heavens. It had become evening and the light was dimming. Yet this gentle rain[9] glistened as it seemed to stay suspended in air, yet ever so slowly, making its way down from the heavens, covering and enveloping all. I stepped out into the dimming day, and into this shroud of golden light. The sensation caressed me. I began to twirl slowly, very slowly, in this gentle rain.[10] Wafting clouds touched, caressed, and then turned to fine gold upon my skin.

My clothing was nothing more than a simple dressing gown[11], but as this rain began to envelop me, my gown began changing before my eyes. Somehow, walking out into this mist, and into the eve of the day, a transformation process began. I had no idea what was about to take place, but I felt the change on my skin, and the difference in my clothing. Everything about my covering was transformed.[12] I was now adorned in beautiful, billowing satin! My hair grew thick, full and luxuriant. Radiant joy burst through my countenance![13]

At the height of the moment, Jesus took my hand and with excited anticipation, led me away. He led me where no other eyes could see us, where no one else was watching. As we moved forward, toward an unfamiliar place, He led me away from the rain and into the growing darkness. As He drew me forward, we walked along the edge of an enormous, dark hedge.[14] I could sense His anticipation, a controlled excitement at what was about to happen.

Far from the pavilion, we passed through an arch in the ominous, green foliage and entered into a murky and foreboding place.[15] I had never seen or felt anything like it. Something like a brown haze hung in the air. I began to feel a weight, as if that murkiness had descended upon my shoulders — not a tangible object, but the pressure of something unseen. It was a weight so heavy I instantly knew there was no way I could bear it. But even as I began to think, *there is no way I can carry this,* from deep within I heard a stern reproof.[16]

Stop! Do not even think that way!

Intuitively I knew that I was not allowed these feelings. *I must carry it, it is my duty to carry it, it is my responsibility to carry it — and I must do it in a worthy manner!*

How do I possibly carry such a load without being bowed completely to the ground? What does this posture look like?

As I thought these things, the Lord paused just inside the arched opening. He bent down and began to do something that amazed me! He began to sew jewels on the hem of my gown.[17] He placed long slender beads of pure gold, alternating with brilliant diamonds. He dusted my gown with small clusters of glittering diamonds and adorned my veil with what seemed like diamond dust. The Lord hung magnificent jewels from the crown that He placed on my head.[18] Then, one by one, my Beloved carefully placed a row of sparkling diamonds just below each of my brow bones, capturing the upper curve of my eyes.[19]

As the Lord completed His work, my dress transformed into the most glorious gown ever seen, with every jewel declaring the majesty and splendor of its Creator! There have never been jewels like these in all of creation and they formed an exquisite picture of loveliness, from the hem to the veil! From the segments of golden piping circling the hem, interspersed with the brilliant stones, to the diamonds covering the dress and veil, all were completely breathtaking! Yet there was something exquisitely mysterious in the image of the multi-colored jewels dangling on my forehead, and the embedded stones on the crown! All completely Glorious![20]

As the Lord placed the last jewel, I was struck with the revelation that He is adorning "His Bride." I became not an individual bride, but a representation of the entire Bride of Christ.

He now turns her shoulders and looks directly into her eyes. Just like a bolt of lightning cutting through darkness, lasting only a moment, His look makes His objective clear. It is intense, complete and pure passion, focused for her! His purpose pierces through her, and He declares, 'You are Mine!!' [21] [22]

Unspoken words follow, as He begins to withdraw from her. She understands — *it is time*. He backs away, eyes locked with His Bride's, never breaking His gaze. His white steed stands ready.[23] He mounts, preparing for His ride, "The Ride at the appointed time", that was for-or-dained to take Him to the place where He will unite with His Beloved. His single purpose is His betrothal to His Bride![24] In a moment in time, He travels far away, thousands of miles, yet never do His eyes break from hers.[25] [26]

But the Bride is now alone. Before her is a long and dark pathway.

She now understands that *for her*, it is time. The gravity and weight of what she must do is enormous. She knows she cannot bear it — but yet she must! It is a very heavy weight,

> *a weight of responsibility,*
> *a weight of love,*
> *a weight of calling,*
> *a weight of denial of self, and*
> *a weight of single focus!*

She must carry herself as His Bride. She must carry the responsibility — her position, her honor, her calling. She must, and so she can!

She dare not fear! She dare not despair. She dare not be ashamed, embarrassed or self-pitying. She cannot be haughty or prideful. It is not her, but the Call of Him that she carries, a call that will strengthen and enable her. She knows this can only be accomplished one way — keeping her gaze locked on His. However far off in the distance, she can still see Him and His eyes are piercing hers. She can only take a step, and each step toward their final destiny, by breathing His name, ...*Jesus...*, *Jesus...*, *Jesus...* with each breath, ...*Jesus!*

Dirt, rocks and stones create a long, dark path before her that winds its way through an ominous throng of onlookers. They are all amazed. They all stand watching.[27] Most are jeering, some are hurling insults, and others observe in stunned silence.[28] But the Bride[29] does not hear them. She barely notices their pursed lips and wagging tongues, as she catches a glimpse of the crowd in the periphery as she walks steadily onward. She is not cognizant of their demeanors or their loathsome expressions because her eyes are locked on her Beloved's. She cannot comprehend their words and they do not penetrate her. She only hears her own words, her Beloved's name formed on her lips, ... *Jesus...*, *Jesus...*, *Jesus....* with each step, Jesus! It is a grave responsibility, to carry the presence of her Beloved within her, into the midst of an angry mob. But now she is full of determination, hope, perseverance and a knowing that she must reach her Beloved. She is His![30]

With each determined and difficult step, the pathway responds.[31] What was a dark and rocky road now responds with bursts of light from beneath her feet! Each step is cushioned as if she walked on the buoyancy of clouds! The pathway springs forth with puffs of gold, bursts of glittering light from beneath each step.[32]   And each step reaffirms her hope. Each step with His name, *Jesus*, on her lips, reaffirms she will carry this responsibility. Her heart bursts with love for her Beloved as she moves forward, deeper and deeper into the darkness and into the jeering crowd.[33] Her eyes are only for Him, set steadfastly upon Him,[34] and every breath is His name, ...*Jesus...*, *Jesus...*, *Jesus...*.

A Voice suddenly resounds through the Heavens, arresting the activities of men, stilling the mob before her as the Father's proclamation rings throughout eternity,

"The Bride has begun her Walk!"[35]

Part 2

Part Two

—·••·—

Will You Respond?

Entering into the presence of the Lord is an experience of unspeakable honor. When the Lord beckons His Intended into His secret chamber, she does not realize His purpose:

He has called her to be His Bride.

> *I WILL CALL THOSE WHO WERE NOT MY PEOPLE, 'MY PEOPLE', AND HER WHO WAS NOT BELOVED, 'BELOVED'.*
>
> Rom. 9:25

In The Vision revealed in Part I, His Beloved is truly experiencing each and every event. She not only witnesses each scene with absolute clarity, but she is actually living in each moment. She feels the passion, the love and the intensity of each experience.

Every part of the vision has depth of meaning. It is not just for you to ponder or contemplate; it is a calling from the Heart of the Father asking you to respond.

He is calling you to accept or reject the depths of His love and bear the responsibility of living your life as the Bride of Christ.

It is a call to respond with, "Yes, Lord!" or, to turn away — unwilling to carry the responsibility. Of course, this Beloved in the Vision represents those who cry, "Yes!" This is a vision of the Bride who does go on to meet her Beloved, arrayed personally by His hand into a work of His glorious splendor!

For those of you whose heart cries *Yes!*, or for those of you whose strongest desire is to say *Yes!*, then you will want to ponder the following detailed account.

In the following pages we will delve into the deeper meaning of this vision. You will hear the call of the Lord in each part. If you say *Yes* to His first request, you will be beckoned to enter in to the next scene and to respond *Yes* yet again! And just as the intimacy increases, so does your desire — and so does your responsibility.

Quietly listen to the voice of His Spirit as you read. You will hear Him calling. You will understand what He desires to impart to you personally.

See yourself entering…

But as for me, by Your abundant lovingkindness I will enter Your house, At Your holy temple I will bow in reverence for You.

Psalm 5:7 NAS

Chapter 1

The Veiled Pavilion

The Lord beckons you into the flowing chiffon pavilion — within the veil.

This hope we have as an anchor of the soul, a hope both sure and steadfast and one which enters within the veil.

Heb. 6:19

Our initial invitation is always by the wooing and drawing of the Holy Spirit. He is full of abundant mercy and grace, which is ever available within His presence. He is drawing you into His presence, into the secret place where just you and He alone will partake of intimate communion.

When you allow yourself to enter in, you will realize that it is here in the secret place of the tent of meeting, the quiet place of prayer and communion with the Lord, where He longs to meet with you — His Beloved.

For in the day of trouble He will conceal me in His tabernacle; In the secret place of His tent He will hide me…

Ps. 27:5

YOU WILL FIND THE VISION — PART 1 ON THE MARGINS OF THE FOLLOWING PAGES. REFRESH YOURSELF WITH THE ORIGINAL VISION AS OFTEN AS NEEDED TO CLEARLY DISCERN YOUR BELOVED'S CALL…

He beckoned me to enter through the heavenly veil. The Lord was standing within a four-cornered pavilion , like the structures that are situated on the beach at the edge of the sea. The roof and walls, made of a white, chiffon fabric, billowed gently in the breeze. Jesus held open the side of the veil closest to me and invited me in. I looked around in awe and, although His words were not audible, His thoughts and intentions were as if spoken. He spoke His Peace, He spoke His Love, and He was amused with me. I was looking around, thoroughly enjoying the environment and all the love and peace He was showering upon me. He kept drawing me toward Him. I so enjoyed this intimacy. But only for a moment. Then I looked around and thought, shouldn't I be doing something? I knew there was so much work to be done, people to minister to, shouldn't I be doing something? The Lord laughed and chuckled. He drew me to Him and communicated to me that I should just rest. But, but,…. Just rest? He smiled.

The Lord beckons to all of us to enter into His chambers, into quiet times of repose with Him. His earnest desire for you is that you secret yourself away with Him so that you are able to hear His voice of love and passion for you.

You may think that the Lord has never called you in this way. You are not alone. Many of us have failed to hear His voice. Even when we do recognize the still small voice of His Spirit drawing us, often we are too distracted to respond. We keep ourselves so busy and our lives so full of noise, that we brush off the quiet whisper of His Spirit. Yet the Lord continues to call,

> **Go therefore to the main highways, and as many as you find there, invite to the wedding feast.**

Matt. 22:9

Then He beckoned me to lie with Him on a chaise lounge, I realize He really means that I should rest, with Him, right next to Him, peacefully immersed in His presence.

He has something so great to share with us, so wonderful that it is beyond our own understanding. And often we do not even comprehend that He is calling! Then if we hear, we wonder what we will possibly do or say when we really enter His presence? What could we have to say to *the* Almighty and Powerful God?

But His gentleness and grace tells us if we will trust Him, and do as He says — coming into His presence and just resting with Him — we will find that all the Heavenly secrets are His and our greatest surprise will be in discovering that He desires to share them with us! He IS the answer to our every question and our every need for affirmation and love.

But, unfortunately, many will never come.

Why? Because we do not understand what this call from the Lord means. We think it means busyness and work. We do not realize that the Lord's call means rest. His call means just being who He created us to be — those who are abiding in His presence. His greatest desire for us is to know Him!

The closest communion we have as humans is the marriage bed, where husband and wife come to know one another at the most intimate level possible as human beings. And just as the groom consummates the marriage with his bride, so the Lord's call to us is to come into the secret place, the quiet place of intimacy with Him, just to know Him and to be known by Him. He wants you to know His deepest desire and His deepest passion is intimacy with you!

As we respond to His calling, there is a covering of protection for us within the secret place of intimacy and provision in every area of our lives. This secret place of intimacy is where He shares His passion for you, and for the world, so that you are able to carry His likeness into the earth! Our very first *Yes!* to Him must be to enter into His secret chambers and rest — resting into knowing and being known by Him in the quiet seclusion of intimate communion. We must decide to lay aside all the things that distract, or even entertain us, for the precious moments alone with Him.

Joy is the evidence that we have entered His rest.

We lay next to each other, He directly behind me, holding me as one holds a child, close and comforting, yet His love was intimate to the heart. I relaxed and enjoyed His presence, and then, again, I thought, I should be doing something. He conveyed through His amusement, that I should enjoy this time and rest. I tried to rest, but I was flighty of thought and fidgety. Gently but firmly, the Lord put His arm around me and placed His hand directly through my chest and upon my heart. He began to massage my heart to beat in rhythm with His. Our hearts beat as one! This was amazing! I instantly entered into His rest.

For we who have believed enter that rest…

Heb. 4:3

Joy comes as we enter into His rest. Never learning to walk in joy has dismal consequences.

Because you did not serve the LORD your God with joy and a glad heart, for the abundance of all things; therefore you shall serve your enemies.

Deut. 28:47

Entering through the veil is the first step in discovering the vast riches the Lord has for those who are His.

…so that in the ages to come He might show the surpassing riches of His grace in kindness toward us in Christ Jesus.

Eph. 2:7

Most of us would readily agree that we want the blessings of an intimate relationship with the Lord. We want provision, comfort, love, peace, rest, and all the fullness of what Christ is to and for us, as is set forth in the Scriptures. Yet even though we desire to be His Bride, being beckoned into the Lord's presence can cause a degree of discomfort. Many wonder, *What will be revealed when I enter into His chambers? What will He see about me that I have so carefully kept hidden?*

Our lives are often a type of masquerade. We are always trying to please Him and others by our carefully chosen words, our outward appearance, and by our "doing" instead of our "being." But in that "being" is the reflection of who He is. To step out of the hustle and bustle of life, and into the unfamiliar place of quiet surrender requires focused discipline and a heart's desire for Him above all else.

But the Lord answered and said to her, "Martha, Martha, you are worried and bothered about so many things; but only one thing is necessary, for Mary has chosen the good part, which shall not be taken away from her."

Luke 10:41-42

We have allowed ourselves to become performance-based even when the Words of our Lord are so clear! The better part is sitting at His feet! His highest calling to us is to love and be loved, and to know true intimacy with Him — not to put on display our works or deeds. He desires that you experience the ultimate relationship — which is only with Him!

A child cannot be conceived unless a man and woman come together in physical intimacy. This is a reflection of the design of Heaven! The Father, through His Son, and by the Holy Spirit, calls you and me into deep spiritual intimacy, where the Lord will bare His heart and show us His designs for us! When we abandon ourselves into His intimate presence, we will conceive the plans and dreams He has decreed for us from the beginning of time.

"I am my beloved's and my beloved is mine…"
"You are as beautiful as Tirzah, my darling, As lovely as Jerusalem,
As awesome as an army with banners."

Song of Solomon 6:3,4

Through this vision we see that our Lord is somewhat amused. Although He laughs and chuckles at our busyness, He continues to woo and draw us to Himself ever hopeful that our response will be a willing *Yes*. Whenever we allow ourselves to be wooed, and we agree to repose with Him, He will take these moments of submission and reveal to us His heart.

I will put My law within them and on their heart I will write it; and I will be their God, and they shall be My people.

Jer. 31:33b

Do you want to please the Lord? Do you want to bring joy to Him, your Beloved? Enter in to His embrace and experience His passion!

The LORD your God is in your midst,
A victorious warrior.
He will exult over you with joy,
He will be quiet in His love,
He will rejoice over you with shouts of joy.

Zeph. 3:17

"I stand at the door and knock" (Rev. 3:20) is the Lord's persistent reminder to us. By His Holy Spirit, He is knocking, calling, and wooing us continually. Yet many will not answer His beckoning call; many will not make themselves ready.

Then the kingdom of heaven will be comparable to ten virgins, who took their lamps and went out to meet the bridegroom. Five of them were foolish, and five were prudent. For when the foolish took their lamps, they took no oil with them, but the prudent took oil in flasks along with their lamps. Now while the bridegroom was delaying, they all got drowsy and began to sleep. But at midnight there was a shout, 'Behold, the bridegroom! Come out to meet him.' Then all those virgins rose and trimmed their lamps. The foolish said to the prudent, 'Give us some of your oil, for our lamps are going out.' But the prudent answered, 'No, there will not be enough for us and you too; go instead to the dealers and buy some for yourselves. And while they were going away to make the purchase, the bridegroom came, and those who were ready went in with him to the wedding feast; and the door was shut. Later the other virgins also came, saying, 'Lord, lord, open up for us. But he answered, 'Truly I say to you, I do not know you. Be on the alert then, for you do not know the day nor the hour."

Matt. 25:1-13

Oil is a precious commodity to the Lord. It signifies here His Beloved's absolute abandon to Him, in complete and 'full' joy and gladness of heart, only realized by His precious Holy Spirit. The oil is the *Yes!* that you speak at every beckoning of His hand, and at every sound of His voice. It is the precious willingness to the call of intimacy! The Virgins who wanted intimacy were ready to enter in. They maintained the appropriate level of readiness and expectancy of intimacy with their Lord. They were ready and able to immediately respond to the sound of His call.

> *You have loved righteousness and hated wickedness; Therefore God, Your God, has anointed You With the oil of joy above Your fellows.*

Ps. 45:7

You see, there are requirements for being invited into the Bridal Chamber. Serving the Lord with the "oil" of joy and gladness is one! Being attentive to His voice at every moment is another! Once you are within the veil, do you know what the Lord requires of you to enter into oneness with Him? Read carefully and examine your heart — the heart He is so willing to conform to His:

> *O LORD, who may abide in Your tent?*
> *Who may dwell on Your holy hill?*
> *He who walks with integrity, and works righteousness, And speaks truth in his heart. He does not slander with his tongue, Nor does evil to his neighbor,*
> *Nor takes up a reproach against his friend; In whose eyes a reprobate is despised, But who honors those who fear the LORD; He swears to his*

own hurt and does not change; He does not put out his money at interest,
Nor does he take a bribe against the innocent.
He who does these things will never be shaken.

Ps. 15:1-5

The Light of the Word of God is shining brightly, showing you the way into His presence. Throughout the Word of God He beckons you into the secret place, where you can know Him and be known by Him. Will you be one who will make yourself ready before His appearing? Or will you be one that will wait? There will be those that wait — those that wait until the thick darkness comes that will so completely cover the earth. Then will there be a cry for intimacy and the light of His secure presence?

THE SUN WILL BE TURNED INTO DARKNESS AND THE MOON
INTO BLOOD, BEFORE THE GREAT AND GLORIOUS DAY OF THE
LORD SHALL COME. AND IT SHALL BE THAT EVERYONE WHO
CALLS ON THE NAME OF THE LORD WILL BE SAVED.

Acts 2:20-21

You may be as one sitting on the fence saying, "I want to want to do right!" and "I want to want to pray!" "I want to want to know Him in an intimate way!" Your desire can change. Your desire can grow. But you must first discover the measure of His great love for you! I John 4:19 sets our thinking straight: "We love, because He first loved us." Run to the secret place and hide right up next to Him! Know Him and be known by Him! Then you will be one that is transformed and you will be one that returns with Him, as His Glorious Army, when He comes for His own on that final day!

And I saw heaven opened, and behold, a white horse, and He who sat on
it is called Faithful and True, and in righteousness He judges and wages

war. His eyes are a flame of fire, and on His head are many diadems; and He has a name written on Him which no one knows except Himself. He is clothed with a robe dipped in blood, and His name is called The Word of God. And the armies which are in heaven, clothed in fine linen, white and clean, were following Him on white horses.

Rev. 19:11-14

His Beloved would never follow Him, and she would certainly never bear the weight of her calling, unless her heart beat as one with His! He knew this was impossible for her to attain on her own. Therefore, by an act of His magnificent love, He himself reached into the depths of her soul and caused her heart to become one with His, as she submitted herself to Him.

I will give my people hearts that are completely committed to me. I will give them a new spirit that is faithful to me. I will remove their stubborn hearts from them. And I will give them hearts that obey me.

Ezek. 11:19 NIRV

Now, this Beloved, the one who has submitted herself into His hands, is no longer concerned about what she should be "doing." She now understands that her goal is "being," in His adoring presence! By His hand, and His hand alone, her heart has been transformed into the likeness of His! The Glory of God is now resident in the core of her being!

*But we all, with unveiled face, beholding as in a mirror the glory of the Lord, are being transformed into the same image from glory to glory, just as from the Lord, the Spirit. *

2 Cor. 3:18

The greatest of gifts awaits you just inside of the veil.

If anyone is thirsty, let him come to Me and drink.

John 7:37b

But you must say, *"Yes!"* and step forward…

Lessons from this chapter:

a. Desire to go where Jesus beckons.

b. Yield to the will of the Lord.

c. Allow His close scrutiny.

d. Allow Him to change you.

e. When you hear His Spirit, move toward Him.

f. Let Him lead your every step.

In the light of a king's face is life, And his favor is like a cloud with the spring rain.

Proverbs 6:15 NAS

May he come down like rain upon the mown grass, Like showers that water the earth. In his days may the righteous flourish,

Psalm 72: 6-7 NAS

Chapter 2

The Rain

Let my teaching drop as the rain,
My speech distill as the dew,
As the droplets on the fresh grass
And as the showers on the herb.
For I proclaim the name of the LORD;
Ascribe greatness to our God!
The Rock! His work is perfect,
For all His ways are just;
A God of faithfulness and without injustice,
Righteous and upright is He.

Deut. 32:2

... and he will cause to come down for you the rain,
the former rain, and the latter rain in the first
month.

Joel 2:23b, KJV

When the rain touches her skin, His Beloved comes alive in spirit, responding without restraint to her Lord!

Are you willing for the rain to fall on you?

From beyond the veil at the opposite end of the pavilion, I heard a voice say, "The rain of God is coming down! Blood and water!" Jesus stood and took me by the hand. He led me through the pavilion and as we reached the opposite side, He removed the veil. What I saw fascinated me — there was wave upon wave of golden mist, floating down from the heavens. It had become evening and the light was dimming. Yet this gentle rain glistened as it seemed to stay suspended in air, yet ever so slowly, making its way down from the heavens, covering and enveloping all. I stepped out into the dimming day, and into this shroud of golden light. The sensation caressed me. I began to twirl slowly, very slowly, in this gentle rain. Wafting clouds touched, caressed, and then turned to fine gold upon my skin. My clothing was nothing more than a simple dressing gown, but as this rain began to envelop me, my gown began changing before my eyes. Somehow, walking out into this mist, and into the eve of the day, a transformation process began. I had no idea what was about to take place, but I felt the change on my skin, and the difference in my clothing. Everything about my covering was transformed. I was now adorned in beautiful, billowing satin! My hair grew thick, full and luxuriant. Radiant joy burst through my countenance.

None of us know how to instinctively walk His walk. We must just begin, by and in His grace. We must put one foot in front of the other, trusting Him. It is a spiritual walk of submission, one we may have never done before, and one we can never do without Him!

When He beckons His Beloved and draws her by the hand into the rain, she trusts Him. She has only learned this trust by spending time in quiet seclusion with Him. Her heart, through His hand, is now beating as one with His. Knowing Him and trusting Him makes her ready to receive the changes that are about to take place. The rain of Heaven, His cleansing streams that now envelop her, begins to remove all remaining pretense! It is the presence of His Holy Spirit, as a soft enveloping mist, that leaves her without defenses and completely at peace!

> *You will make known to me the path of life; In Your presence is fullness of joy; In Your right hand there are pleasures forever.*
>
> *Psalm 16:11*

When she steps into the rain and begins to turn, ever so slowly in the fine mist, the rain caresses her being and there is absolutely no discomfort. Her yielding displaces every barrier of resistance and all hardness of heart falls away.

> *So let us know, let us press on to know the LORD. His going forth is as certain as the dawn; and He will come to us like the rain, like the spring rain watering the earth.*
>
> *Hosea 6:3*

Some of us do not like the rain. I, for one, would rather be watching the mist through my picture window within my cozy living room. Rain tends to ruin my hair and causes spots on my clothing. One would rarely expect a good outcome from standing in a rushing deluge! Some of us feel the same way toward our Lord's cleansings — they seem uncomfortable and exposing. We think that if our facades are jeopardized we will be left feeling inferior and unacceptable. We fear no longer appearing "together." We fear that removal of our manicured and well-maintained veneer will reveal the true "(wo)man behind the curtain."

Yet the Lord has paid a great price, in His own Blood, to 'wash' His Beloved.

> *Blessed are those who wash their robes, so that they may have the right to the tree of life, and may enter by the gates into the city.*
>
> *Rev. 22:14*

Certainly, in His presence, when we put aside all our charades and yield to the Holy Spirit, there are no feelings of inferiority and no feelings of shame. There are absolutely no feelings of helplessness and no feelings of inadequacy. When we allow the Lord to remove our "grime" and to wash us and fill us with who He is, He transforms us into His likeness at that moment! When we yield ourselves to the Lord, He completely changes our lowliness into His Royalty! He will never leave us naked and uncovered!

> *For our citizenship is in heaven, from which also we eagerly wait for a Savior, the Lord Jesus Christ; who will transform the body of our humble state into conformity with the body of His glory, by the exertion of the power that He has even to subject all things to Himself.*
>
> *Phil. 3:20-21*

Purification and sanctification are processes that occur one step at a time, and one decision at a time. As we progress and each decision is yielded to the Lord, we are changed. As His Beloved wholly abandons herself to the cleansing rain, a transformation begins to takes place.

Purify me with hyssop, and I shall be clean; Wash me, and I shall be whiter than snow.

Psalm 51:7

Sanctify them in the truth; Your word is truth.

John 17:17

Only those who will yield to His washing with His Word, who will allow the application of His Word to their hearts and lives, will be conformed to His image. This requires a removing of everything from ourselves that is contrary to the knowledge and will of God.

We are destroying speculations and every lofty thing raised up against the knowledge of God, and we are taking every thought captive to the obedience of Christ.

2 Cor. 10:5

When we submit in this way to the Lord's cleansing rain, we are purified and we are enabled to walk in that purity. The Lord's rain is a covering of fine gold, representing this purity!

Now he made the room of the holy of holies ... and he overlaid it with fine gold.

2 Chron. 3:8

The "Holy of Holies" was the innermost chamber of the Tabernacle, the secret place where the most holy sacrifice of blood was placed for cleansing of sin. Jesus, our Christ, placed His own blood on this altar, once for all, for our eternal purification and reuniting to the Father. In this "Holy of Holies" there is room for only one priest to stand before the Lord in worship. Under this covering of gold, purity is declared. This secret place of intimacy with the Father, by the Blood of Jesus, and through the power of the Holy Spirit, is the place of transformation of our souls in intimate worship.

> *But you are A CHOSEN RACE, A ROYAL PRIESTHOOD, A HOLY NATION, A PEOPLE FOR GOD'S OWN POSSESSION, so that you may proclaim the excellencies of Him who has called you out of darkness into His marvelous light.*
>
> *1 Peter 2:9*

In this posture of intimacy, we no longer strive to be beautiful, handsome, or appreciated by people, we have become "altogether lovely" to our Lord. He is not looking for sacrifice any longer, what He requires is obedience. When we are no longer concerned with our apparel, what others think of our appearance, our beliefs, or other superfluous things, we are able to give our all in service and relationship to our Lord.

> *It was given to her to clothe herself in fine linen, bright and clean; for the fine linen is the righteous acts of the saints.*
>
> *Rev. 19:8*

The young woman who had stepped into the white-chiffon pavilion, had now been transformed — from Glory to Glory. (2 Cor. 3:18)

What is "Glory?" The character and likeness of our God! We are transformed as one aspect of the character of our God builds upon another.

Now her heart, having been captured by Him within the veil, within His secret place of communion, is set to follow Him! She has been cleansed to follow Him, having submitted herself to the washing of the Word and the purification of her soul!

...so that He might sanctify her, having cleansed her by the washing of water with the word...

Eph. 5:26

So that now, even into the night, into the twilight, she will follow Him.

I am the light of the world. Those who follow me will never walk in darkness. They will have the light that leads to life.

John 8:12, NIRV

Lessons from this chapter:

a. Allow the Lord to woo you to repentance.

b. Submerse yourself in Him, the Living Word.

c. Continue applying the Word until He becomes who you are.

d. Do not be shocked at the transformation that will take place.

e. Allow Him to lead you, no matter the circumstances.

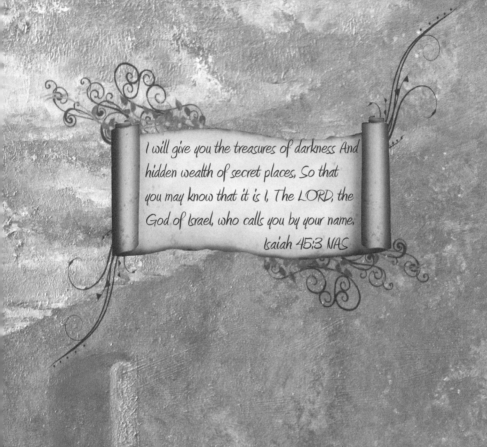

I will give you the treasures of darkness And
hidden wealth of secret places, So that
you may know that it is I, The LORD, the
God of Israel, who calls you by your name.

Isaiah 45:3 NAS

Chapter 3

• • • •

Twilight

He leads her by the hand and she is not afraid.

Behold, God is my salvation, I will trust and not be afraid; For the LORD GOD is my strength and song, And He also has become my salvation.

Isa. 12:2

When your heart is completely captured by your Beloved, you are not concerned about the darkness. You look forward to your new life of intimacy and adventure before you. Your Beloved leads you, running into the night, and you follow, giddy at the adventure. Suddenly, a wall of separation lies between what you have previously lived and the new experiences which lie ahead.

Imagine entering into a dimension that you have never known. As His Beloved steps through the arched entry, she steps into an unfamiliar region. Like a distortion in time and space, she finds herself in a place she has never experienced before. Immediately she realizes there is profound purpose in what is happening. Yet a mounting sense of heaviness bears down upon her. She begins to feel a weight, a denseness to the air, and a

At the height of the moment, Jesus took my hand and with excited anticipation, led me away. He led me where no other eyes could see us, where no one else was watching. As we moved forward, toward an unfamiliar place, He led me away from the rain and into the growing darkness. As He drew me forward, we walked along the edge of an enormous, dark hedge. I could sense His anticipation, a controlled excitement at what was about to happen. Far from the pavilion, we passed through an arch in the ominous, green foliage and entered into a murky and foreboding place. I had never seen or felt anything like it. Something like a brown haze hung in the air. I began to feel a weight, as if that murkiness had descended upon my shoulders - not a tangible object, but the pressure of something unseen. It was a weight so heavy I instantly knew there was no way I could bear it. But even as I began to think, there is no way I can carry this, from deep within I heard a stern reproof.

Stop! Do not even think that way!

Intuitively I knew that I was not allowed these feelings. I must carry it, it is my duty to carry it, it is my responsibility to carry it — and I must do it in a worthy manner! How do I possibly carry such a load without being bowed completely to the ground? What does this posture look like?

49

pressure she has not previously known. Her first instinct is to run; but she knows she dare not leave her Lord. She notices her breathing is labored and the weight and pressure upon her is difficult to bear. She wants to stop and throw herself to the ground in defiance of what she feels is about to happen. She looks to hide beneath something, anything, that will keep her from this pressure.

But there is nowhere to go.

…Lord, to whom shall we go? You have words of eternal life.

John 6:68

There is such pressure — so many thoughts and so many feelings, that an overwhelming sensation of interminable helplessness shrouds her.

Even when I walk
through the darkest valley,
I will not be afraid,
for you are close beside me.
Your rod and your staff
protect and comfort me.

Psalm 23:4, NLT

From the time we were little children, our parents and caregivers have encouraged and persuaded us to persevere. We have been told "You can do it!" … "Keep going!" And so, we have mustered up our strength and pushed and tried and did it again, until we actually accomplished what we thought was an impossible feat. As we grew, we constructed patterns and methods, and ingrained them so that many behaviors we now do are by rote. We have been there and done that before, so these hurdles present as non-issues to us. But when it comes to our *calling*, the rules are not the same.

Spiritual battles and spiritual accomplishments require spiritual posture.

So now, we have the Hosts of Heaven encouraging us with their shouting, "You can do it!" … "Keep going!" — but we must know what this looks like and what it is we are to do!

The Apostle Paul gave us a wonderful example in Galatians 2:20:

I have been crucified with Christ; and it is no longer I who live, but Christ lives in me; and the life which I now live in the flesh I live by faith in the Son of God, who loved me and gave Himself up for me.

Knowing the Lord in intimacy is a covenant relationship. Covenant means, "All I have for all He has. All I am for all He is." It is a complete exchange. In Christ, He takes all of us: our sin, shame, unworthiness, weaknesses — all of us, in exchange for all of Him: His strength, ability, purity, power, might, righteousness, holiness, love, peace — all of His character now residing within us!

His call to us is to learn to draw upon all of His attributes now resident within us! He has seeded each of these attributes within us through covenant, and as we draw upon them, we grow into His likeness. His burning desire is for us to understand and grow into our proper posture, which is our position hidden in Him!

For you have died and your life is hidden with Christ in God.

Col. 3:3

Whenever and wherever He leads us, He knows full well that we are able to go the distance. He knows, and yet we do not. With all of the pressures and responsibilities we sense, we waiver. But because He is the one who has prepared us AND set the path that is before us, He leads. And we go, one step at a time, one decision at a time. This requires a knowing and a trusting in Him, so that as long as we stay postured (hidden) in Him, we are able.

Now through the archway, the Lord leads His Beloved. He knew exactly where He was leading her, into a dimension completely devoid of faith. He led her into thick darkness and oppression — absent of all spiritual understanding.

> *Blow a trumpet in Zion,*
> *And sound an alarm on My holy mountain!*
> *Let all the inhabitants of the land tremble,*
> *For the day of the LORD is coming;*
> *Surely it is near,*
> *A day of darkness and gloom,*
> *A day of clouds and thick darkness.*
>
> *Joel 2:1-2a*

The Lord has a plan for His Beloved. He has always provided her needs, and even in this hour of gloom and darkness, His miraculous preparation of her and for her continues.

> *"They will be Mine," says the LORD of hosts, "on the day that I prepare My own possession, and I will spare them as a man spares his own son who serves him. So you will again distinguish between the righteous and the wicked, between one who serves God and one who does not serve Him".*
>
> *Mal. 3:17-18*

She pushes her feelings aside, in wonder of her Lord as she is led into this dismal place, inside the foreboding hedge. She has gone through a transformation of the very core of her being and she has learned to follow her Lord faithfully. She is still ignorant of what the deepening darkness holds for her on this dark side of the massive divide. She has no understanding of this dimension, yet all the inhabitants there are anticipating her arrival.

And she follows…

Lessons from this chapter:

a. See Jesus with you at all times and in every circumstance.

b. When you do not understand His leading, go anyway.

c. Crucify your soul daily and yield to who He is, resident within you.

d. Always hold fast to Him in the process.

e. Do not entertain thoughts contrary to His Word and Truth.

f. Ask, and He will show you the way.

I am overwhelmed with joy in the Lord my God! For he has dressed me with the clothing of salvation and draped me in a robe of righteousness. I am like a bridegroom in his wedding suit or a bride with her jewels.

Isaiah 61:10 NLT

Chapter 4

Adornment

Just inside the hedge, in this new dimension, their progress ceases. The Lord knows His Beloved cannot advance further without suitable preparation.

She is astonished when He stoops down and painstakingly begins to sew precious jewels onto the hem of her dress. One after another, He works to encircle her feet with a halo of sparkling beads. She focuses on her breathing, and she is still trying to maintain her posture. The heaviness is ever-present, and yet her attention begins to be drawn toward the work of her Lord. As her focus shifts to His work, her feelings wane. She becomes fascinated with how devoted He is to His task. It becomes apparent that He is creating not just pretty ornamentation; — He is preparing her, covering her, for what is ahead, an event which is to come.

As I thought these things, the Lord paused just inside the arched opening. He bent down and began to do something that amazed me! He began to sew jewels on the hem of my gown. He placed long slender beads of pure gold, alternating with brilliant diamonds. He dusted my gown with small clusters of glittering diamonds and adorned my veil with what seemed like diamond dust. The Lord hung magnificent jewels from the crown that He placed on my head. Then, one by one, my Beloved carefully placed a row of sparkling diamonds just below each of my brow bones, capturing the upper curve of my eyes.

As the Lord completed His work, my dress transformed into the most glorious gown ever seen, with every jewel declaring the majesty and splendor of its Creator! There have never been jewels like these in all of creation and they formed an exquisite picture of loveliness, from the hem to the veil! From the segments of golden piping circling the hem, interspersed with the brilliant stones, to the diamonds covering the dress and veil, all were completely breathtaking! Yet there was something exquisitely mysterious in the image of the multi-colored jewels dangling on my forehead, and the embedded stones on the crown! All completely Glorious!

…just as He chose us in Him before the foundation of the world, that we would be holy and blameless before Him."

Eph. 1:4

He knows He must personally provide everything for her; to make her who she is to become. He would not think to let another do His work. As He sews and places precious jewels and stones upon her gown, she realizes the precise and perfect love that is the intention of His every move.

… and to present her to Himself as a radiant church, without stain or wrinkle or any other blemish, but holy and blameless".

Eph. 5:27, NIV

There is a secret concerning the jewels which the Lord has placed upon her crown. She does not realize it, but the Lord knows it very well — she has earned each one. The carefully placed diamonds on her brow line and the magnificent jewels embellishing her crown are the evidence of her righteous deeds! They are the evidence of acts, which she has accomplished in His name, acts that were focused on those His heart cries out to redeem! By her every *Yes* to Him, she has lived as His hands extended to a desperately ill world, and she has made herself ready for every act of service in His name.

"Lift up your eyes and look around; All of them gather together, they come to you. As I live," declares the LORD, "You will surely put on all of them as jewels and bind them on as a bride".

Is. 49:18

His likeness now covers her in every aspect; every part of her has been transformed into a reflection of His radiant beauty!

For no man can lay a foundation other than the one which is laid, which is
Jesus Christ. Now if any man builds on the foundation with gold, silver,
precious stones, wood, hay, straw, each man's work will become evident;
for the day will show it because it is to be revealed with fire, and the fire
itself will test the quality of each man's work. If any man's work which he
has built on it remains, he will receive a reward.

I Cor. 3:11-14

The ornamentation of His Beloved's attire is the final revelation of her righteous service to her Lord. And He is sure to anchor each jewel securely to her stunning gown. Each stone, each bead, represents her submission to the character of her Lord. She has allowed who He is to be worked into every facet of who she is.

And they shall be mine, saith the LORD of hosts, in that day when I make
up my jewels…

Mal. 3:17, KJV

Each stone and each bead has specific purpose and meaning. Golden beads exemplify her purification. Just as golden nuggets are purified by fire, we also are purified through every choice we make, to walk in such a way as to reflect the character of Christ.

He will sit as a smelter and purifier of silver, and He will purify the sons
of Levi and refine them like gold and silver, so that they may present to the
LORD offerings in righteousness.

Mal. 3:3

Notice the Lord's exquisite provision for His Bride — this adornment, a suspended circle surrounding her feet. These stones are almost indestructible and the strongest gem on earth, so no matter where she must walk, no harm will come. Diamonds represent stability, brilliancy, virtue and right-standing with God. These same gems frame her eyes, her vision, allowing her to see only Him in all that she does. A complete shield of protection covers her, as evidenced in the adornment of the diamond dust layering her entire gown.

> *Strength and dignity are her clothing, And she smiles at the future.*
>
> *Prov. 31:25*

She has allowed her Lord to cover her, and He has become her strength! Strength which will keep her through every event that lies ahead!

> *The LORD is my strength and song, And He has become my salvation…*
>
> *Ex. 15:2a*

The Lord has also covered her by placing a golden crown to encircle her head. The golden halo signifies purity of mind and thought which have been captured by and belong to her Lord. She is His and her thoughts will wander to nothing and no one else!

> *Therefore, the woman ought to have a symbol of authority on her head…*
>
> *1 Cor. 11:10*

The jewels suspended from her crown and covering her forehead have very special significance. These are representative of the character of her Christ, woven intricately through her thinking and decision making processes. She wears them with dignity and honor.

It is important to appreciate the origin of these precious stones: jasper, sardis, emeralds, rubies, sapphire, and amethyst. They originate in the Kingdom of Heaven! These stones are an expression of the character of our God. Everything that He has made in His Kingdom is in His likeness and emanates from His perfection. These stones represent each aspect of His character.

Some stones are firm, and solid, unmovable — just as He is. These attributes are represented by gems like the diamond and the sapphire. Stones such as the emerald and ruby are somewhat softer, and represent the steadfast tenderness of the Lord toward us. Amethysts represent the color of royalty and splendor, befitting His royal priesthood. Sardis and Jasper are foundational stones, a representation of His ownership and redemption of "our land" (who we are), which is His precious possession.

As His Beloved views her glorious covering, despite this dark place of uneasiness and lack of understanding, the knowledge of her position becomes clear. She now comprehends that she is indeed "His Bride." The purpose of her attire and adornment becomes a realization — she has a position to fill and a work to accomplish. She is not yet sure what it is, but she understands, that for the Lord himself to painstakingly clothe and adorn her, there surely is a purpose for His work!

Then one of the seven angels … spoke with me, saying, "Come here, I will show you the bride, the wife of the Lamb." And he carried me away in the Spirit to a great and high mountain, and showed me the holy city, Jerusalem, coming down out of heaven from God, having the glory of God. Her brilliance was like a very costly stone, as a stone of crystal-clear jasper."

Rev. 21:9-11

Do you know this to be true for you? Are you aware of the high calling the Lord Himself has placed upon you in this last hour? He has adorned you to carry His royalty and His likeness into this world, a very dark place. But as you go, as you walk into this darkness, His jewels, His attributes, will reflect the brilliance of His light and His likeness, through you, and into the gloom and despair which is the atmosphere of the world in which we live.

Lessons from this chapter:

a. Without question, go where the Lord leads.

b. Believe, without a doubt, that He will prepare you for what is ahead.

c. Preparation requires "being still".

d. Adornment (anointing) is reflective, it is not for the Bride alone.

e. Seek His illumination, you will not know your calling without it.

A Vision of the Jewels

I entered a large room, painted entirely white. The white walls flowed upwards into a white ceiling, and even the floor gleamed white. Covering the floor, from corner to corner, lay sparkling jewels, so large that they were the size of the palm of my hand. I could barely enter the room. There were so many stones that I had nowhere to step without injuring my feet.

The Lord stood just inside the room. I thought to ask Him, "Lord, what are these stones?" His answer was not what I expected to hear. I thought He would explain that these were the Gifts of the Spirit as written in 1 Cor. 12, but He did not.

He answered and said, "These are the righteous acts of the saints."

I instantly knew what He meant. These were the works of those who were His, the works of those that had come before me and others of our time. These precious, radiant stones represented writings, sermons, books, paintings, research and study of the Word – all the Revelation that His precious saints had memorialized throughout time, to reach a lost and dying world. Again, I posed a question, "Lord, what do I do with them?"

And the Lord spoke gently, "Give them to the people." Then more forcefully He declared, "The gifts are for the people! Give them to the people!"

I bent down and gathered as many as I could hold and as I passed by the Lord, ready to do as He had instructed, He again said, "Sandra! The gifts are for the people! Give them to the people!"

And I understood what He meant – take the work that has been done before, all that has been laid out, the hours of research, prayer, teaching, writing – these are great gifts and they are to be used in this hour! Take them, distribute them, give them, teach them, share them! There is no time to waste! The gifts, the gleaming jewels, are for the people to see! They are for the people's benefit! The people must see and partake of these gifts in these final hours in time! And there is no time to waste!

They will be mine," says the LORD Almighty, "in the day when I make up my treasured possession. I will spare them, just as in compassion a man spares his son who serves him.

Malachi 3:17 NIV

How sweet is your love, my treasure, my bride! How much better it is than wine! Your perfume is more fragrant than the richest of spices.

Song of Solomon 4:10 NLT

I am my beloved's, And his desire is for me.

Song of Solomon 7:10 NAS

Chapter 5

You are Mine!

His piercing gaze cut through every thought and every fear His Bride entertained. There is nothing that can overshadow His penetrating and possessive stare. It cuts through pretense and posture, and bores through to the very marrow of our existence.

Imagine your chiefest desire — whether it is being loved and experiencing intimacy to the very core of your being, or whether it is being admired for your stalwart stand for Godliness and justice. The Lord alone fulfills your desire in every facet, in every way!

The Lover of your soul comes to you and fills you with His sure and complete acceptance, passion, belonging, and His conquering Love!

Whether you are male or female, every one of us has longings and desires in the deepest parts of our being. I am not speaking of sexual desires and sensual urges, but the deepest longings of purpose, existence, and personhood that a human being may have. One look from the Lord satisfies and fulfills, and then

> As the Lord placed the last jewel, I was struck with the revelation that He is adorning "His Bride." I became not an individual bride, but a representation of the entire Bride of Christ. He now turns her shoulders and looks directly into her eyes. Just like a bolt of lightning cutting through darkness, lasting only a moment, His look makes His objective clear. It is intense, complete and pure passion, focused for her! His purpose pierces through her, and He declares, "You are Mine!" Unspoken words follow, as He begins to withdraw from her. She understands – it is time. He backs away, eyes locked with His Bride's, never breaking His gaze. His white steed stands ready. He mounts, preparing for His ride, "The Ride at the appointed time", that was for-ordained to take Him to the place where He will unite with His Beloved. His single purpose is His betrothal to His Bride! In a moment in time, He travels far away, thousands of miles, yet never do His eyes break from hers.

binds you to that eternal purpose that He has created just for you! Look into His eyes!

The declaration, "You are Mine!" leaves no question and no insecurities. There is no room for introspection or preparation. It is a statement of authority and a statement of finality.

With this statement "You are Mine!" comes responsibility. You must step out of what you have known and step into the present and eternal purpose God predestined you to carry! You are, at this moment in time, at the place where everything you have been purposed for meets everything you will be. You have come to the point of relinquishment of all, so that you may receive all that there is for you. There is not one speck of doubt that can remain at this moment of His Holy infusion of Life, Truth, and Purpose into your being. His eyes are piercing to your very core and contain a passion that you have never known!

He is speaking Isa. 43:1 to you: You are no longer your own; you have been chosen to be His for eternity.

Do not fear, for I have redeemed you; I have called you by name; you are Mine! When you pass through the waters, I will be with you; And through the rivers, they will not overflow you. When you walk through the fire, you will not be scorched, Nor will the flame burn you. For I am the LORD your God, The Holy One of Israel, your Savior; I have given Egypt as your ransom, Cush and Seba in your place. Since you are precious in My sight, Since you are honored and I love you, I will give other men in your place and other peoples in exchange for your life.

Isa. 43:1b–4

There is a moment when we realize, it is time: time to move on or time to stop; time to rest or time to go forward. There are moments throughout our lives where we know a shift has occurred. Like a revolving door, one moment you are inside, and the next moment you are outside in a completely different atmosphere, in an unknown environment — and here, there is no going back.

When His gaze is so intense upon us, so full of passion, His image is branded upon our hearts and on our minds. There is no way we can go back to the little we had known before. We can never return. The door is closed and our life has been changed forever. Our only choice is to move forward.

For this is the covenant I will make with them, after those days says the Lord, I will put my laws upon their hearts and write them on their minds, and I will be their God and they shall be My people.

Heb. 8:10

When the Lord places His law in our hearts, it is so we will walk in righteousness to be a light, a standard, for the world around us. He wants you to shine by allowing His character to shine through you!

And yet, this Bridegroom is leaving. Where is He going? To take His position. He is to begin His final approach to meet His Beloved! It is at the Father's appointed time! He has a job to do, as does His Bride!

He is leaving her alone. And yet, His eyes are locked on hers. No matter how far away He travels, His eyes of possessive passion are still upon hers. It is not even possible that she will not follow Him. It is sealed, it is done. She belongs to Him and He is her King, her Lord, and her Beloved!

And I saw heaven opened, and behold, a white horse, and He who sat on it is called Faithful and True, and in righteousness He judges and wages war. His eyes are a flame of fire, and on His head are many diadems; and He has a name written on Him which no one knows except Himself. He is clothed with a robe dipped in blood, and His name is called The Word of God. And the armies which are in heaven, clothed in fine linen, white and clean, were following Him on white horses. From His mouth comes a sharp sword, so that with it He may strike down the nations, and He will rule them with a rod of iron; and He treads the winepress of the fierce wrath of God, the Almighty. And on His robe and on His thigh He has a name written, "KING OF KINGS, AND LORD OF LORDS."

Rev. 19:11-16

Lessons from this chapter:

a. You are His — your life is not your own!

b. Allow Him to love every part of you, to the depths of your soul.

c. Realize the Godly desires you have are placed within you by Him.

d. Things will change, allow the 'shift' to take place.

e. You have now become His likeness to a lost world.

f. Take your place and see His glory!

Your anointing oils are fragrant; your name is oil poured out . . . Draw me after you; let us run. The king has brought me into his chambers. We will exult and rejoice in you; we will extol your love more than wine; rightly do they love you.

Song of Solomon 1:3-4 ESV

Chapter 6

She Steps Forward

The Bride is now alone. The atmosphere around her is only gloom and despair. There is a deep brown haze all about. Others are there, but they are not like her. Here the individuals are full of torment, full of anger, jeering, maligning, hostile, and full of hatred. She sees the path before her winds directly through the raucous mob. Heaviness pushes down on her. Can she even breathe?

She calls out, *Jesus!* And there is air. *Jesus!* And there is strength. *Jesus!* And she begins to understand.

She remembers her Lord's words:

Do not fear, for I have redeemed you; I have called you by name; you are Mine! When you pass through the waters, I will be with you; And through the rivers, they will not overflow you. When you walk through the fire, you will not be scorched, Nor will the flame burn you. For I am the LORD your God, The Holy One of Israel, your Savior.

Isa. 43:1b–3a

But the Bride is now alone. Before her is a long and dark pathway. She now understands that for her, it is time. The gravity and weight of what she must do is enormous. She knows she cannot bear it — but yet she must! It is a very heavy weight, a weight of responsibility, a weight of love, a weight of calling, a weight of denial of self, and a weight of single focus! She must carry herself as His Bride. She must carry the responsibility - her position, her honor, her calling. She must, and so she can! She dare not fear! She dare not despair. She dare not be ashamed, embarrassed or self-pitying. She cannot be haughty or prideful. It is not her, but the Call of Him that she carries, a call that will strengthen and enable her. She knows this can only be accomplished one way - keeping her gaze locked on His. However far off in the distance, she can still see Him and His eyes are piercing hers. She can only take a step, and each step toward their final destiny, by breathing His name, . . . Jesus . . ., Jesus . . ., Jesus . . . with each breath, . . . Jesus!

If she is to meet her Beloved, if she is to be betrothed to Him for eternity, she must walk forward. She must carry herself properly! Not with her head hung in fear and trepidation, not with her chin jutting forward in haughty disregard and pride, but squared, even regal, as is becoming of His Bride.

...I... implore you to walk in a manner worthy of the calling with which you have been called...

Eph. 4:1

Do you see yourself as His Bride? Do you see yourself as the one He gave everything to eternally possess? Then this is the time you must know who you are and whose you are. You must not look back. You must not look back to attempt to assess your situation, or to see how you have made it this far. To be called His Bride you must have previously counted the cost! You have entered an intimate relationship with your Lord and you have conceived His desirous love for you. Turning back or changing your mind abort the plans He has for you!

We often look at our natural circumstances and decide, *this is not possible.* We limit His life and power within us by our natural thinking. But it is now past the time of decision making. You have pledged to be His; you have pledged your life to Him and you have yielded every part of your soul

Dirt, rocks and stones create a long, dark path before her that winds its way through an ominous throng of onlookers. They are all amazed. They all stand watching. Most are jeering, some are hurling insults, and others observe in stunned silence. But the Bride does not hear them. She barely notices their pursed lips and wagging tongues, as she catches a glimpse of the crowd in the periphery as she walks steadily onward. She is not cognizant of their demeanors or their loathsome expressions because her eyes are locked on her Beloved's. She cannot comprehend their words and they do not penetrate her. She only hears her own words, her Beloved's name formed on her lips. . . . Jesus. . ., Jesus. . .., Jesus. . .. with each step, Jesus! It is a grave responsibility, to carry the presence of her Beloved within her, into the midst of an angry mob. But now she is full of determination, hope, perseverance and a knowing that she must reach her Beloved. She is His!

to His plan and purpose for you. Now you must carry the Will of God within you!

The Lord says, "Break forth! ... Step forward... Trust Me!" Do you hear Him? Or do you only hear the wicked and cursing crowd that surrounds you?

Alone in the encroaching gloom, the Bride turns. As the darkness appears to rise around her, the Bride prepares to take her first step. It will be a step into darkness and into the unknown, like stepping off a cliff into utter nothingness. Yet, the light of her Lord's eyes spanning across eternity stay locked upon her. She can "see", when her eyes are locked with His. Breathing is another matter. The only air in this sullen and oppressive place is that contained in His Name, "*Jesus!*" So she must breathe Him in. She must not look at what is going on around her, or she will lose the only illumination she has. She dare not listen to the oppressive crowd, or she will lose the words of life on her own lips. Focus! Complete and absolute focus must be her posture!

> *A highway will be there, a roadway, And it will be called the Highway of Holiness. The unclean will not travel on it, But it will be for him who walks that way, And fools will not wander on it.*
>
> *Isa. 35:8*

But her Beloved makes it easy. Fixed on His passionate stare, hearing His precious name whispered again and again from her own lips, holds the Bride in His peace. She trusts Him. She has learned to believe.

> *Trust in the LORD with all your heart and do not lean on your own understanding. In all your ways acknowledge Him, And He will make your paths straight.*
>
> *Prov. 3:5-6*

When the Lord speaks His Word to our hearts, it does not always take root. Sometimes our hearts are hard and stony — there is no place for hope to plant! In our best times, we receive His Word joyously! After all, it is our Lord who is speaking to us, and we recognize His voice! That in and of itself is a miracle!

But even then there are occasions where we begin to waiver. When we share our excitement with others and receive less than an enthusiastic response, we may then begin to compare what we have heard from Him to what others are saying. Quickly, we begin to wonder, *was that really the Lord?* In a short time we convince ourselves that we were mistaken, there was no "Word" and we are just deluding ourselves.

Fortunately, there are other times when we just hold fast and grow stronger as a result. We know it is Him! We hear His voice! We actually hear Him telling us His plan for us! We know what we must do! We know we must respond! We must go and accomplish what the Lord has called us to do! It is special, it is exciting, and He asked *me* to do it.

With each determined and difficult step, the pathway responds. What was a dark and rocky road now responds with bursts of light from beneath her feet! Each step is cushioned as if she walked on the buoyancy of clouds! The pathway springs forth with puffs of gold, bursts of glittering light from beneath each step. And each step reaffirms her hope. Each step with His name, Jesus, on her lips, reaffirms she will carry this responsibility. Her heart bursts with love for her Beloved as she moves forward, deeper and deeper into the darkness and into the jeering crowd. Her eyes are only for Him, set steadfastly upon Him, and every breath is His name, . . . Jesus. . ., Jesus. . ., Jesus. . ..

We decide we will follow Him, to the very ends of the earth — right after we finish our schooling. Or maybe it is a house we are building. Or just as soon as we get a job, or a different job, or quit our job. And then, when our own conditions are not met, we let go of the excitement, the hope and the dream of doing something big for God. Our shortsightedness has blinded us. We could not see a way or a path through all the things we feel we must do in the world, and so we give up.

But to His Bride, to the soldier, to the one who has given everything and given up everything; for the one that has put his or her hand to the plow and has not looked back (Luke 9:62), there is Light! You see it and you follow it. There is nowhere else to go. Jesus has the words of eternal life. Jesus is the reason you live. Jesus is the reason you breathe. Jesus IS your hope!

> *Let us hold fast the confession of our hope without wavering, for He who promised is faithful.*
>
> *Heb. 10:23*

Now you begin to unload every pack, trunk, and overcoat. Every burden, possession and relationship that causes you to stumble in your walk with Him, you remove. You begin to exercise the hope within you. You begin to pray the Word He has given you. You pray the vision that you see. You pray when there is no one else to pray with. You work when no one will work with you. And you see His joy, and His eyes upon you, and you see His smile. You become fully aware that He is there — right with you, at every moment, joining in the experiences of your day. You are sustained with His Words, His presence, and His pleasure with you. Nothing will turn you back!

> *Therefore, since we have so great a cloud of witnesses surrounding us, let us also lay aside every encumbrance and the sin which so easily entangles us, and let us run with endurance the race that is set before us.*
>
> *Heb. 12:1*

And now the Bride takes her first step into the darkness. She trusts Him even though she has no idea what she is walking into. The deep gloom, a jeering crowd, and intense anger permeate the air — yet she still steps forward, eyes locked with her Bridegroom.

To her amazement, upon the Bride's first step, the path immediately responds! Light shoots forth! Golden purity bursts forth! Her steps are miraculously illuminated!

Your word is a lamp to my feet And a light to my path.

Ps. 119:105

Not just light, for bursts of gold dust spring up from the dark ground and illuminate her feet!

But the path of the righteous is like the light of dawn, That shines brighter and brighter until the full day.

Prov. 4:18

The Bride understands that the Lord has made a way for her, even in the darkness. That her footsteps will be sure, for they are encompassed in golden purity. He has made provision for her in advance! There is nothing to fear. The path He has set before her responds with His directives.

For You light my lamp; The LORD my God illumines my darkness.

Ps. 18:28

She must just take each step, one step at a time, breathing His lovely name and looking intently into His commanding eyes!

Behold, I will do something new, Now it will spring forth; Will you not be aware of it? I will even make a roadway in the wilderness, Rivers in the desert.

Isa. 43:19

As the Bride begins to walk, the final moments of time begin.

A Voice resounds through the Heavens, arresting the activities of men, and the Father's proclamation rings throughout eternity,

"The Bride has begun her Walk!"

Lessons from this chapter:

a. Following your Beloved will sometimes feel lonely.

b. He calls to you and woos you into each place.

c. Do not decide your level of obedience by what is occurring around you.

d. Leave everything behind that is not birthed from your intimacy with Him.

e. Walk in His strength and dignity, worthy of your Royal calling.

f. Realize there is no turning back.

g. You ARE His Beloved!

Therefore, since we are surrounded by such a great cloud of witnesses, let us throw off everything that hinders and the sin that so easily entangles. And let us run with perseverance the race marked out for us, fixing our eyes on Jesus, the pioneer and perfecter of faith. For the joy set before him he endured the cross, scorning its shame, and sat down at the right hand of the throne of God. Consider him who endured such opposition from sinners, so that you will not grow weary and lose heart.

Hebrews 12:1-3 NIV

Chapter 7

The Final Sprint

Though the Vision ends with the Father's Proclamation, the scene is pregnant with the realization of what is to come.

Christ's Bride is in full step with the Will of her Beloved. His gaze never leaves her and His decree, "You are Mine!" still rings throughout the heavens. The crowd knows this. Most of them hate the Truth which is now invading their atmosphere, in this dark and dismal environment in which they have brooded for years. Truth is a blinding light, and they would rather have darkness.

> *In Him was life, and the life was the Light of men. The Light shines in the darkness, and the darkness did not comprehend it.*
>
> *John 1:4-5*

The crowd continues to jeer, spit, curse and yell as the Bride makes her way through the mob. She maintains her posture — every breath being His name, "*Jesus!*" She keeps her eyes on her Beloved's; His piercing stare spanning the miles.

> *Let your light shine before men in such a way that they may see your good works, and glorify your Father who is in heaven.*
>
> *Matt. 5:16*

The Bride is not allowed to focus on the crowd, the darkness, or the rocky path. Her charge is to bring light into this place. She carries the countenance of her Lord as she, in complete submission, moves forward for all eyes to see.

> *Blessed are the peacemakers, for they shall be called sons of God.*
> *Blessed are those who have been persecuted for the sake of righteousness,*
> *for theirs is the kingdom of heaven.*
> *Blessed are you when people insult you and persecute you, and falsely say*
> *all kinds of evil against you because of Me. Rejoice and be glad, for your*
> *reward in heaven is great.*
>
> *Matt. 5:9-12*

If you are the Bride, if you have answered *Yes* to every step as you have journeyed along the way, then you know what your posture must be — you must walk through this world, in these last days, adorned in His splendor! You must walk in a manner that will only bring glory to His name (Eph. 4:1).

> *…with gentleness correcting those who are in opposition, if perhaps God*
> *may grant them repentance leading to the knowledge of the truth.*
>
> *2 Tim. 2:25*

Though the world insults the Bride, calling her a fool, hypocrite, liar (or worse), His true Bride will never look down on the lost in pride, nor cower in shame and humiliation — neither action is becoming of the Bride of Christ. We must carry His Message, His Truth, down the dark path of the final hours of history, in regal submission to the Will of our King. It is for the sake of the world, this lost and dying world, that we follow Him in obedience. He gave His life to save us all.

Deliver (rescue) those who are being taken away to death,

And those who are staggering to slaughter, Oh hold them back.

If you say, "See, we did not know this,"

Does He not consider it who weighs the hearts?

And does He not know it who keeps your soul?

And will He not render to man according to his work?

Prov. 24:11-12

Believers in Jesus hold two positions; The Bride of Christ and Soldier in the Army of God. In our position as the Bride, we are completely unified as One in His Spirit.

But the one who joins himself to the Lord is one spirit with Him.

1 Cor. 6:17

As a Soldier in His Army, we also battle the enemy and his cohorts on many different levels. We must become His Bride, totally transformed into His likeness, in order to become a Victorious Warrior in His Army.

For in the day of trouble He will conceal me in His tabernacle;

In the secret place of His tent He will hide me;

He will lift me up on a rock.

And now my head will be lifted up above my enemies around me,

And I will offer in His tent sacrifices with shouts of joy;

I will sing, yes, I will sing praises to the LORD.

Hear, O LORD, when I cry with my voice,

And be gracious to me and answer me.

When You said, "Seek My face," my heart said to You,

"Your face, O LORD, I shall seek."

…Teach me Your way, O LORD,

And lead me in a level path

Because of my foes.

Do not deliver me over to the desire of my adversaries,

For false witnesses have risen against me,

And such as breathe out violence.

I would have despaired unless I had believed that I

would see the goodness of the LORD

In the land of the living.

Wait for the LORD;

Be strong and let your heart take courage;

Yes, wait for the LORD.

Ps. 27:5-14

Do know this, intimacy is required before He will entrust us to conquer!

It was given to her to clothe herself in fine linen, bright and clean; for the fine linen is the righteous acts of the saints.

Rev. 19:8

And the armies which are in heaven, clothed in fine linen, white and clean, were following Him on white horses.

Rev. 19:14

With the Father's final proclamation, the end of time has begun! The Bride has started down the aisle and there is no turning back. How long will it take for the Bride to traverse the walkway? Only the Father knows. But He has shared with us a glimpse of where we are in the culmination of worldly events — the Bride's walk has begun and the Marriage of all time is about to take place!

Many will see, repent, and join the Bride in her walk; many more will fall away. Of those that call themselves "His" and are awaiting His return, there will be as many asleep at the time of His coming as there will be awake and longing for His return!

Five of them were foolish, and five were prudent. For when the foolish took their lamps, they took no oil with them,…Now while the bridegroom was delaying, they all got drowsy and began to sleep. But at midnight there was a shout, "Behold, the bridegroom! Come out to meet him…" And while they were going away to make the purchase, the bridegroom came, and those who were ready went in with him to the wedding feast; and the door was shut. Later the other virgins also came, saying, "Lord, lord, open up for us." But he answered, "Truly I say to you, I do not know you." Be on the alert then, for you do not know the day nor the hour.

Matt. 25:2- 13

The staying power in the walk of the Bride is in being one with her Lord — hidden completely in Him. The key to becoming the Bride and to returning as a Mighty Warrior with Him on that final day, is to understand our hiding place, our place of complete surrender, that place of oneness in Him.

But now I come to You; and these things I speak in the world so that they may have My joy made full in themselves. I have given them Your word; and the world has hated them, because they are not of the world, even as I am not of the world. I do not ask You to take them out of the world, but to keep them from the evil one. They are not of the world, even as I am not of the world. Sanctify them in the truth; Your word is truth. As You sent Me into the world, I also have sent them into the world. For their sakes I sanctify Myself, that they themselves also may be sanctified in truth. I do not ask on behalf of these alone, but for those also who believe in Me through their word; that they may all be one; even as You, Father, are in Me and I in You, that they also may be in Us, so that the world may believe that You sent Me. The glory which You have given Me I have given to them, that they may be one, just as We are one; I in them and You in Me, that they

may be perfected in unity, so that the world may know that You sent Me,
and loved them, even as You have loved Me.

John 17:13-23

If you do not yet know the Father, His Son Jesus, and the precious Holy Spirit — the Triune God, the Holy Spirit is inviting you to become acquainted with the salvation that is available to you through the death and resurrection of the Lord, Jesus the Christ.

There are four points of understanding in receiving the free gift of salvation:

1. Conviction of sin: the understanding that one is a sinner.

2. Repentance: a turning away from sin.

3. Asking the Father, in the name of Jesus, for forgiveness of sin.

4. Make a commitment to Jesus to receive Him as the Lord of your life.

"Lord" is a term many do not understand. From the Greek it means, "possessor, master, sovereign prince, chief, the one to whom someone belongs." In receiving salvation, it is a covenant exchange, everything you are for everything He is. He will then be seated on the throne of your life as Lord and Savior. All that He has will be yours!

If you have never asked Jesus to be the "Lord" of your life, as noted above, the following is a model prayer of surrender to Him. Praying in this manner will allow you to receive Jesus as Lord of your life and thereby making you an heir of Salvation:

Father God, I come to you in the name of Jesus. I acknowledge to You that I am a sinner, and I am sorry and repent for (turn away from) my sins and the life that I have lived; I need your forgiveness.

I believe that Your only begotten Son, Jesus Christ, shed His precious blood on the cross at Calvary and died for my sins, and I am now willing to turn away from my sin and follow Your Word completely.

You said in Your Holy Word, in Romans 10:9, that if I confess with my mouth Jesus as Lord, and believe in my heart that You, Father God, raised Him from the dead, I will be saved.

So right now I confess Jesus as Lord, which means I bow my knees before Him and give Him everything I am. With my heart, I believe that God raised Jesus from the dead. This very moment I accept Jesus Christ as my Savior and according to His Word, I know right now I am saved. I know right now I have the life of Jesus Christ dwelling in me. He freely gave me His life, and I give Him all of mine without reservation.

Thank you Jesus for your unlimited grace which has saved me from my sins. I thank you Jesus that your grace never leads to further sin, but rather it always leads to repentance. Therefore Lord Jesus, transform my life so that I may bring glory and honor to You alone and not to myself. Thank you Jesus for dying for me and giving me eternal life.

Amen! (which means "so be it!")

If you have just now come to know Our Lord Jesus, may I make a suggestion? Begin this book again
you will see things from an entirely new perspective!

If you have known the Lord Jesus, but are just now realizing your responsibility as His Beloved, you too may want to start this book again. See how tenderly He leads you into intimacy with Him, in a place where He alone can make your heart beat as one with His.

See yourself entering the heavenly veil. . ..

You are the light of the world. A city set on a hill cannot be hidden; nor does anyone light a lamp and put it under a basket, but on the lampstand, and it gives light to all who are in the house. Let your light shine before men in such a way that they may see your good works, and glorify your Father who is in heaven.

Matt. 5:14-17

Who is this who looks down like the dawn, beautiful as the moon, bright as the sun, awesome as an army with banners?

Song of Solomon 6:10 ESV

"Warrior Bride"
by Constance Woods

Constance Woods

Chapter 8

The End of This Book
But the Beginning of Eternity

Let us rejoice and be glad and give the glory to Him, for the marriage of the Lamb has come and His Bride has made herself ready.

Rev. 19:7

The Spirit and the Bride say, "Come," And let the one who hears say, "Come" And let the one who is thirsty come; let the one who wishes take the water of life without cost.

Rev. 22:17

Then He said to me, "It is done. I am the Alpha and the Omega, the beginning and the end. I will give to the one who thirsts from the spring of the water of life without cost. He who overcomes will inherit these things, and I will be his God and he will be My son. But for the cowardly and unbelieving and abominable and murderers and immoral persons and sorcerers and idolaters and all liars, their part will be in the lake that burns with fire and brimstone, which is the second death."

Rev. 21:6-8

And the twenty-four elders, who sit on their thrones before God, fell on their faces and worshiped God, saying, "We give You thanks, O Lord God, the Almighty, who are and who were, because You have taken Your great power and have begun to reign!"

Rev. 11:16-17

A Note from the Author

Thank you for taking the time to read *Say, "Yes!"*. My desire was to share the vision as accurately as possible. I have endeavored to do that to the best of my ability. I pray as you have read it that it has encouraged you and stirred you to go deeper with Him as we await His soon coming return.

I would love to hear from you. Please feel free to write to me at:

7380 Olympia Ave
Suite 159
Tulsa, OK 74132

Also, our ministry, God's E.R. is about ministering to those in need of spiritual, physical, and emotional healing. Let me ask you, are you and all the people you care about:

- 100% spiritually free, at liberty and walking in peace?

- 100% emotionally whole and free of emotional pain, and at peace with who you are?

Jesus intends for us to be 100% whole as revealed in Acts 13:39 ... and through Him, everyone who believes is freed from ALL things!

Experience the classes and individual ministry by joining us from your own home and online media device.

Visit: www.GodsER.us for more information on God's E.R.

About the Author

Sandra Williamson has a Master of Arts degree in Human Relations and—along with her husband, James—is the co-founder of the ministry, God's E.R. The Williamsons' goal is to bring *Emergency Restoration* and spiritual freedom to the lives of participants based upon the foundation of Acts 13:39, which states, "…through Him, everyone who believes is freed from ALL things." God's E.R. is a division of Standard Ministries, Inc., which emphasizes the importance of the Word of God as being the standard.

Sandra is a wife, mother of two, stepmother of two, grandmother of two, and spiritual mother to hundreds. Her love for people compels her to pour out her life for others just as she does to her beloved Jesus.

As a young Catholic schoolgirl, Sandra heard the audible voice of God speak from the heavens above the playground, "I have a special work for you to do!" Through many years of searching to know God, her journey took many roads and was wrought with many distractions from the enemy, which were intended to prevent her from discovering the answers to her quest.

After total surrender of her life to Jesus, Sandra has learned to hear His voice and continues to grow in her understanding of His nature, leading, and deliverance. Through this journey, she has received many prophetic insights and visions, one of which she shares here for the benefit of the body of Christ. Her desire is that you will allow Jesus to reveal His heart to you as you experience the intimacy of this vision.

Sandra and her husband make their home in Tulsa, Oklahoma.

About God's E.R. Program

The God's E.R. program is a structured program that facilitates healing and freedom of the spirit, soul, and body. "E.R." in this case, means "Emergency Restoration," which is the foundation of the ministry — restoration to the person that God has always decreed us to be — Freed from All Things (Acts 13:39).

Sandra Williamson is the Executive Director of Standard Ministries, Inc., operating as God's E.R. Sandra has quite a testimony of deliverance and freedom. Her life is a demonstration of emotional healing, a journey in which she emerged from layers of emotional wounds.

The Lord led Sandra to build the God's E.R. program for the purpose of helping the body of Christ understand their position in Him and the freedom that He died for us to attain. The Lord has given Sandra a specific program of ministry, built on a compilation of research, teachings and writings. When facilitated in the E.R. format, this ministry brings such release, forgiveness, and freedom to the participants that even physical ailments are healed!

The program consists of an introductory class and a group cleansing prayer, followed by personal ministry to assist the individual with specifics from their own life. When individuals participate in God's E.R., they are asked to complete a "Problem List" that contains over 340 different problems an individual may be experiencing. Many of these issues have led to emotional problems, criminal behavior or other serious problems in their lives. Though problems and experiences vary greatly, the solutions in each case are very similar. Jesus died that we might be Freed from All

Things, and the Word of God, when consumed and applied, works to change lives!

After all ministry sessions are accomplished, removing layers of emotional wounds, the "Staying Free" class is begun. This eight-lesson class is designed to help the participants obtain the tools to maintain their new-found freedoms. Lesson titles include: Right Thinking, Right Speaking, Choices, Love Yourself, and others.

Subsequent to this class is an additional eight-lesson class entitled "Basic Training for Christians". This class is offered to help each individual find his or her place in the Body of Christ/Army of God. Lesson titles include: Armor of God, Covenant, Plugging into Purpose, Humility, and others.

The objective of this ministry is to assist in facilitating freedom from strongholds and healing of the soul for each participant by means of Scripture and application. The goal is to help the participant be free of former patterns by renewal of the mind and teaching right thinking, right speaking, and making right choices (Eph. 4:22-25).

The methodologies are simply Scripture. The teachings are simply the Word of God. The program relies solely on the Lord as He has spoken through the Scriptures — learning to put them deep into the heart, and guarding them protectively. The only way to believe Scripture in this way is to believe in, and have the most personal of relationships with, the One who died to restore us to the Father — Jesus Christ. The Word works, and therefore all of the methodologies of God's E.R. are based on His Word.

The ministry's on-site location at Victory Christian Center, Tulsa, Oklahoma, also hosts a Healing Room offering targeted prayer for physical healing.

God's E.R. has several additional programs, including a program at the Tulsa Dream Center. God's E.R. is also present in the Oklahoma Department of Corrections. Training sessions for ministry leaders are provided monthly in Tulsa, Oklahoma and by invitation in other cities.

God's E.R. is also working with several Human Trafficking groups to free individuals from the emotional and mental ties to human trafficking.

There are many, many testimonies which cannot be shared due to the ministry's 100% confidentiality position, the only exception being what participants volunteer to share publicly. However, healing and freedom for just about anything you might imagine, from emotional wounds from childhood, to rape, incest, addictions, and witchcraft, have been realized through God's E.R.

God's E.R. has additional ministry for breaking ties to secret societies, removing idols, curses, and other bondages that are not in line with the Word of God. More information may be found online at www.GodsER.us.

It is the hope of God's E.R. that you will find this information helpful and that you will take advantage of the truths set forth in this ministry so that you and those you care about will be Freed from All Things!

Contact us at:
Info@GodsER.us
www.GodsER.us
918.409.8349

About Wings of Mercy Art

Constance Woods is a worshiper, psalmist, and prophetic artist. Her desire and calling is "to heal the brokenhearted, proclaim liberty to the captives, give beauty for ashes, the oil of joy for mourning, and the garment of praise for the spirit of heaviness, that Jesus Christ may be glorified." (Isa. 61.)

Her digital paintings reflect artistic journeys, not only in the crafting but also resulting from her walk through life. Illustrating what God has been speaking and revealing through visions is what distinguishes her as a prophetic artist. The art carries His anointing; therefore, just viewing it touches and impacts many people. Each image conveys a unique story and contains a powerful message within it.

Constance is the founder of both Streams of Mercy Ministry and Wings of Mercy Art. Her original prophetic art is for sale in the form of fine-art prints and canvases in various sizes. Constance also has a line of Scripture fine-art cards. Collections include: Warrior Bride; Lion of Judah; Bride of Christ; Dance; Wings; Eagles; Worship; and Prophecy and Israel.

Through her art, Constance desires to help Christians understand their identity as Christ's bride as well as the relevance of praying for Israel and the Jewish people. Experiencing miracles that God has performed in her family has given her an even deeper love for God and a message that brings hope for all. She and her husband, Woodrow, live in a suburb north of Dallas, Texas.

For additional information on her art you may contact Constance at:

3003 Jacob Drive
Wylie, TX 75098
940-783-1081
www.WingsofMercyArt.com

To purchase additional copies of this book or the accompanying artwork visit our website at

www.GodsER.us

ENDNOTES

1 **Matthew 25:1** *Then the kingdom of heaven will be comparable to ten virgins, who took their lamps and went out to meet the bridegroom.*

2 **Psalm 15:1-5** *O LORD, who may abide in Your tent? Who may dwell on Your holy hill? He who walks with integrity, and works righteousness, And speaks truth in his heart. He does not slander with his tongue, Nor does evil to his neighbor, Nor takes up a reproach against his friend; In whose eyes a reprobate is despised, But who honors those who fear the LORD; He swears to his own hurt and does not change; He does not put out his money at interest, Nor does he take a bribe against the innocent. He who does these things will never be shaken.*

3 **Matthew 22:9** *Go therefore to the main highways, and as many as you find there, invite to the wedding feast.*

4 **Psalm 27:5a** *For in the day of trouble He will conceal me in His tabernacle; In the secret place of His tent He will hide me;*

5 **Matthew 11:29** *Take My yoke upon you and learn from Me, for I am gentle and humble in heart, and YOU WILL FIND REST FOR YOUR SOULS.*

6 **Song of Solomon 1:4** *Draw me, we will run after thee: the king hath brought me into his chambers: we will be glad and rejoice in thee, we will remember thy love more than wine: the upright love thee. (KJV)*

7 **Job 5:10-11** *He gives rain on the earth And sends water on the fields, So that He sets on high those who are lowly, And those who mourn are lifted to safety.*

8 **1 John 5:8** *the Spirit and the water and the blood; and the three are in agreement.*

9 **Proverbs 16:15** *In the light of a king's face is life, And his favor is like a cloud with the spring rain.*

10 *Hosea 6:3* So let us know, let us press on to know the LORD. His going forth is as certain as the dawn; And He will come to us like the rain, Like the spring rain watering the earth.

11 *Isaiah 64:6* But we are all as an unclean thing, and all our righteousness are as filthy rags. (KJV)

12 *2 Cor. 3:18* But we all, with unveiled face, beholding as in a mirror the glory of the Lord, are being transformed into the same image from glory to glory, just as from the Lord, the Spirit.

13 *Psalm 34:5* They looked to Him and were radiant, And their faces will never be ashamed.

14 *Song of Solomon 1:4a* Draw me after you and let us run together!

15 *Isaiah 60:2* For behold, darkness will cover the earth And deep darkness the peoples; But the LORD will rise upon you And His glory will appear upon you.

16 *Isaiah 26:16-19* O LORD, they sought You in distress; They could only whisper a prayer, Your chastening was upon them. As the pregnant woman approaches the time to give birth, She writhes and cries out in her labor pains, Thus were we before You, O LORD. We were pregnant, we writhed in labor, We gave birth, as it seems, only to wind. We could not accomplish deliverance for the earth, Nor were inhabitants of the world born. Your dead will live; Their corpses will rise. You who lie in the dust, awake and shout for joy, For your dew is as the dew of the dawn, And the earth will give birth...

17 *Revelation 21:2* And I saw the holy city, new Jerusalem, coming down out of heaven from God, made ready as a bride adorned for her husband.

18 *Ephesians 5:26-27* To make her holy, cleansing her (as) by the washing with water through the Word, and to present her to Himself as a radiant church, without stain or wrinkle or any other blemish, but holy and blameless. (NIV)

19 **Isaiah 49:16-18** Behold, I have inscribed you on the palms of My hands; Your walls are continually before Me. Your builders hurry; Your destroyers and devastators Will depart from you. Lift up your eyes and look around; All of them gather together, they come to you. As I live," declares the LORD, "You will surely put on all of them as jewels and bind them on as a bride."

20 **Song of Solomon 1:9-11** To me, my darling, you are like My mare among the chariots of Pharaoh. Your cheeks are lovely with ornaments, Your neck with strings of beads. We will make for you ornaments of gold with beads of silver.

21 **Song of Solomon 4:9** You have stolen my heart, my sister, my bride; you have stolen my heart with one glance of your eyes, with one jewel of your necklace. (NIV)

22 **Isaiah 43:1-4** But now, thus says the LORD, your Creator, O Jacob, And He who formed you, O Israel, "Do not fear, for I have redeemed you; I have called you by name; you are Mine! When you pass through the waters, I will be with you; And through the rivers, they will not overflow you. When you walk through the fire, you will not be scorched, Nor will the flame burn you. For I am the LORD your God, The Holy One of Israel, your Savior; I have given Egypt as your ransom, Cush and Seba in your place. Since you are precious in My sight, Since you are honored and I love you, I will give other men in your place and other peoples in exchange for your life.

23 **Revelation 19:11** And I saw heaven opened, and behold, a white horse, and He who sat on it is called Faithful and True, and in righteousness He judges and wages war.

24 **Song of Solomon 3:11** Go forth, O daughters of Zion, And gaze on King Solomon with the crown With which his mother has crowned him On the day of his wedding, And on the day of his gladness of heart.

25 **Psalm 11:4,7** The LORD is in His holy temple; the LORD'S throne is in heaven; His eyes behold, His eyelids test the sons of men. For the LORD is righteous, He loves righteousness; The upright will behold His face.

26 **Psalm 104:1-3** *Bless the LORD, O my soul! O LORD my God, You are very great; You are clothed with splendor and majesty, Covering Yourself with light as with a cloak, Stretching out heaven like a tent curtain. He lays the beams of His upper chambers in the waters; He makes the clouds His chariot; He walks upon the wings of the wind…*

27 **Isaiah 61:10-11** *I will rejoice greatly in the LORD, My soul will exult in my God; For He has clothed me with garments of salvation, He has wrapped me with a robe of righteousness, As a bridegroom decks himself with a garland, And as a bride adorns herself with her jewels. For as the earth brings forth its sprouts, And as a garden causes the things sown in it to spring up, So the Lord GOD will cause righteousness and praise To spring up before all the nations.*

28 **Isaiah 6:10** *Render the hearts of this people insensitive, Their ears dull, And their eyes dim, Otherwise they might see with their eyes, Hear with their ears, Understand with their hearts, And return and be healed.*

29 **Revelation 21:9-11, 18-30** *Then one of the seven angels … spoke with me, saying, "Come here, I will show you the bride, the wife of the Lamb." And he carried me away in the Spirit to a great and high mountain, and showed me the holy city, Jerusalem, coming down out of heaven from God, having the glory of God. Her brilliance was like a very costly stone, as a stone of crystal-clear jasper. The material of the wall was jasper; and the city was pure gold, like clear glass. The foundation stones of the city wall were adorned with every kind of precious stone. …And the street of the city was pure gold, like transparent glass. I saw no temple in it, for the Lord God the Almighty and the Lamb are its temple. And the city has no need of the sun or of the moon to shine on it, for the glory of God has illumined it, and its lamp is the Lamb. The nations will walk by its light, and the kings of the earth will bring their glory into it. In the daytime (for there will be no night there) its gates will never be closed; and they will bring the glory and the honor of the nations into it; and*

nothing unclean, and no one who practices abomination and lying, shall ever come into it, but only those whose names are written in the Lamb's book of life.

30 **Revelation 22:17** The Spirit and the bride say, "Come." And let the one who hears say, "Come." And let the one who is thirsty come; let the one who wishes take the water of life without cost.

31 **Psalm 119:105** Your word is a lamp to my feet And a light to my path.

32 **Proverbs 4:18** But the path of the righteous is like the light of dawn, That shines brighter and brighter until the full day.

33 **Revelation 7:9-14** After these things I looked, and behold, a great multitude which no one could count, from every nation and all tribes and peoples and tongues, standing before the throne and before the Lamb, clothed in white robes, and palm branches were in their hands; and they cry out with a loud voice, saying, "Salvation to our God who sits on the throne, and to the Lamb. And all the angels were standing around the throne and around the elders and the four living creatures; and they fell on their faces before the throne and worshiped God, saying, "Amen, blessing and glory and wisdom and thanksgiving and honor and power and might, be to our God forever and ever. Amen." Then one of the elders answered, saying to me, "These who are clothed in the white robes, who are they, and where have they come from?" I said to him, "My lord, you know." And he said to me, "These are the ones who have come out of the great tribulation, and they have washed their robes and made them white in the blood of the Lamb."

34 **Hebrews 12:2** Looking unto Jesus the author and finisher of our faith; who for the joy that was set before him endured the cross, despising the shame, and is set down at the right hand of the throne of God. (KJV)

35 **Revelation 19:7-9a** Let us rejoice and be glad and give the glory to Him, for the marriage of the Lamb has come and His bride has made herself ready. It was given to her to clothe herself in fine linen, bright and clean; for the fine

linen is the righteous acts of the saints. Then he said to me, "Write, 'Blessed are those who are invited to the marriage supper of the Lamb.'"

Revelation 19:14 *And the armies which were in heaven followed him upon white horses, clothed in fine linen, white and clean. (KJV)*